CONTENTS

Lloyd's Register and the Health and Safety Executive have been pleased to assist The Engineering Council by sponsoring the publication of its *Code of Professional Practice* and the *Guidelines on Risk Issues*. The *Code* and *Guidelines* are intended to help engineers to discharge their responsibilities in these vital and challenging areas. They will emphasise to those who employ or work with engineers the importance of the professional technical input to the control of risk. The *Code* and *Guidelines* make recommendations which will greatly assist all parties as they develop their policies on matters related to risk.

WHAT IS RISK?

There are many definitions of risk. Three are offered below:

RISK is the chance of an adverse event.

RISK is the likelihood of a hazard being realised.

A technical definition:

RISK is the combination of the probability, or frequency of occurrence of a defined hazard and the magnitude of the consequences of the occurrence.* It is therefore a measure of the likelihood of a specific undesired event and its unwanted consequences or loss.

---

* Definition in accordance with BS 4778

See Appendix 4 for references and bibliography. See *Appendix 5* for a glossary of other terms.

I INTRODUCTION

The *Code of Professional Practice on Engineers and Risk Issues* (the Code), which became effective from 1 March 1993, applies to the 290,000 registrants of The Engineering Council. It is reproduced in Appendix 8 for information. These *Guidelines on Risk Issues* will however, be of assistance to everyone interested in risk (see Figure 1). They contain background information to help engineers* and all interested parties to gain a fuller understanding of the Code and how it can be implemented. It should be noted that the Guidelines do not form part of the Code and are not enforceable under the Bye-Laws of The Engineering Council. A complementary initiative on *Engineers and the Environment* is currently being developed by The Engineering Council.

FIGURE 1   *Interested Parties in Risk Issues*

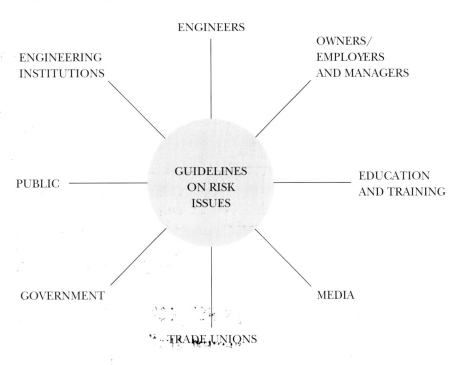

The Guidelines are written as an overview to some of the issues raised in the Code for those who may be less familiar with recent developments. The intention is to provide practical and ethical guidance on risk issues. The Guidelines are neither a technical code of practice nor a manual for risk management. The Bibliography includes a list of relevant publications from individual Institutions and organisations which contain a more detailed treatment of the subject.

It is recognised that the levels of understanding, practice and responsibility for risk issues vary widely. The Engineering Council's booklet *Recommended Roles and Responsibilities* may also be helpful.

The structure of the Guidelines follows that of the Code itself. It starts with an overview of the legal and professional constraints on the engineer, followed by an introduction to the concepts underlying risk management, and finishes with a discussion of the implications for education and public awareness. However, before the 10 points of the Code are discussed in turn, there is a general discussion of the perception of risk which is followed by a list of suggested implementation actions.

---

* The term 'engineer' is used throughout and includes all Engineering Council registrants, namely Chartered Engineers, Incorporated Engineers and Engineering Technicians.

II PERCEPTION OF RISK

Any hazard may to some degree present a risk to the health and safety of people, the environment or the activity (see Figure 2):

- Risks to the health and safety of people include personal injury and in the extreme, loss of life. Thus 'safety' in this context is taken to be freedom from unacceptable risks of personal harm.

- Risks to the environment include pollution, damage to flora and fauna (plants and animals) and soil erosion.

- Risks to the activity include damage to equipment, loss of output, resultant contractual delays and penalties.

FIGURE 2   Engineering Risk Factors

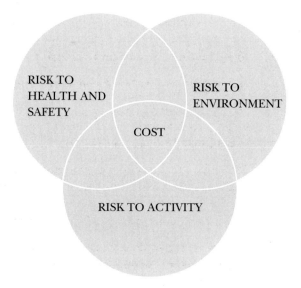

These three different risk factors are connected together by a cost factor. This determines how much money, time and effort should be spent to bring them to acceptable levels. Engineers therefore have the challenging role of balancing these risk factors.

Engineering risk assessment is based on objective consideration of likelihood and consequences. However, individuals and often organisations have to make judgements based on their perceptions of likelihood and consequences. Thus, the absence of a common framework for evaluating risks can make it difficult to arrive at consensus decisions.

Risks are perceived differently according to their scale and nature, and not by simply multiplying the frequency and consequences. A 1 in 100 chance per year of a major accident injuring 100 people has a different significance from 1 fall per year injuring 1 person, for instance, even though the average injury rate per year is the same. This reflects an aversion which is attached by society to major accidents or dread consequences, e.g. cancer.

Other factors which influence the perception of risk include the degree of trust in the organisation; familiarity and understanding of the technology; the extent of involvement in the decision making process; whether it is believed that more could be done to reduce risk; comparisons with accepted risks; and – last but not least – the fairness in the distribution of the risks and benefits. A more exhaustive list is contained in Reference 4. Engineers need to appreciate these factors because they directly influence judgements as to the level of risk that an individual or society considers acceptable or tolerable (see *Appendix 5, Glossary*). These different perceptions mean that there is scope for confusion in communicating with the public and non-specialists on risk issues, and great care needs to be taken.

III SUGGESTED IMPLEMENTATION ACTIONS

Owners, employers/managers, registered engineers, professional Institutions, providers of education and training, trade unions, government, The Engineering Council, the media and the public are all affected by risk issues. These parties are urged to review their current practices in relation to the guidance promoted in the Code and Guidelines and take action accordingly.

Owners/Employers and Managers
(see also Table 2, 'Profile of Good Management Practice' in Guideline 7, page 20)

Lead by commitment to creating, implementing and monitoring a risk management policy which is integral with business policy.

Create a proactive cultural awareness of risk issues at corporate and at the individual level.

Introduce a systematic approach e.g. through Total Quality Management (TQM). Train personnel to give them appropriate skills and knowledge (includes all engineers and technicians in risk awareness training).

Adopt a confidential blame-free accident reporting system.

Engineers

Apply the Code in your professional role.

Understand risk issues associated with your work and the company's policy on risk matters.

Keep up to date with risk assessment and risk management issues through continuing professional development (CPD).

Communicate relevant information on risk issues to those who need to know (e.g. employers/managers, operators, colleagues and the public).

Professional Institutions

Promote the new Code on a local, national and international basis.

Make provision to deal with enquiries which may arise from members and where necessary refer exceptional enquiries to The Engineering Council in accordance with agreed procedures.

Encourage local society meetings to discuss 'identification, assessment and management of risk', lessons from good and bad practice, and how your members can implement the Code.

Encourage members to be up to date in risk assessment and management by inclusion of appropriate initial education and continuing professional development.

The Board for Engineers' Registration (which comprises nominees from engineering Institutions) and its associated committees is asked to play a leading role in the introduction of risk assessment and management in initial and continuing education and training for engineers.

Providers of Education and Training
(including educational establishments, professional Institutions, employers, trade unions, and associations which provide education and training)

Encourage an awareness of risk issues in young people's education (e.g. in primary and secondary schools) with help from the Neighbourhood Engineers scheme as appropriate.

Provide a general awareness of risk issues for all engineers during their initial formation.

Identify needs and provide regular updating in risk assessment and management as part of continuing professional development (CPD) for engineers post registration.

Encourage research and development in the recognition, assessment and management of engineering risks and disseminate the findings.

Review curricula of existing courses relevant to *Engineers and Risk Issues* in the light of current and changing future needs.

Trade Unions　Encourage and support employers to adopt good practice in risk assessment and management.

Promote the benefits of systematic risk management and safe behaviour amongst your members.

Support and encourage your members to seek improved education and training in risk awareness, assessment, management and associated health and safety legislation.

Government　In the regulatory role (e.g. HSE, CAA) use influence and resources to support and follow best practice and explore new ways to improve awareness and practice of risk management by goal setting and other proactive approaches.

Set an example by requiring all engineers entering and already in government service to follow best practice in risk management, and in its role as a customer, to require suppliers to follow best practice.

Provide financial and other incentives to stimulate employers, individual engineers and others to gain greater knowledge and skills in risk awareness, assessment and management by improved education and training to meet present and future needs.

The Engineering Council　Continue to promote the Code and Guidelines locally, nationally and internationally through articles, talks, seminars and conferences. Involve Engineering Council Regional Offices (ECROs), Neighbourhood Engineers and CPD advisers appropriately.

Set up a help line to deal with exceptional queries relating to the Code and other associated issues referred through Institutions or directly.

Continue to bring about a more positive attitude towards engineers and risk issues amongst employers, professional Institutions, providers, trade unions and individual engineers.

Publicise and encourage industry to adopt good practice in risk issues (e.g. through the example set by Industry Affiliate companies).

Give leadership to providers and encourage inclusion of risk awareness, assessment and management in initial and continuing education and training/professional development of all engineers.

Media　Recognise your influence and responsibility by keeping technical risk issues in perspective.

Consult with experts in the engineering profession on technical risk issues.

Help educate the public and technical audiences on technical risk issues by stimulating debate and running informed features/programmes.

Support and help publicise initiatives by engineering bodies and others which identify good practice.

The Public　Seek information from local industry and from the services which you use to
(see also Guideline 10)　demonstrate that risk to the public has been assessed properly, and that an adequate risk management programme is in place.

Encourage engineers to speak at public meetings, discussions, seminars and conferences to promote public awareness of risk issues.

IV GUIDELINES ON RISK ISSUES

1. PROFESSIONAL RESPONSIBILITY

A member of the engineering profession knowingly and voluntarily undertakes a responsibility to others within the community, and in so doing, shoulders certain personal, social and professional obligations. This responsibility to society is widely recognised, particularly in respect of risk issues, and is reflected in the various Codes of Conduct set out by the professional engineering Institutions and The Engineering Council.

The purpose of these Guidelines is to take these general codes as a starting point and to comment on the practical implications of the responsibility owed by engineers in respect of risk issues, and to provide specific guidance to resolve risk concerns satisfactorily (see also *Guideline 3, Resolving a Risk Concern, page 12*). Because of their involvement and understanding, engineers have a central role in the control of risk. Their professional duty rightly includes the exercise of competence and integrity. However, individual engineers alone cannot generally be held responsible for protecting society from risk; those with managerial accountability must also bear some responsibility.

In setting out these practical implications, the Guidelines recognise and draw engineers' attention to the importance of the other influences which should govern their conduct. *Guideline 2, The Law* below therefore briefly discusses the implications for conduct within the existing legal framework, and *Guideline 3, Conduct (page 11)* expands on the requirements of professional codes. Mention is also made of the implications for personal or commercial insurance in *Guideline 2, The Law. Guideline 8, Evaluation (page 21)* provides guidance on forming a judgement about the tolerability of risk.

2. THE LAW

This section gives an introduction to aspects of the law which are relevant to engineers and risk issues. It is not a formal legal treatise; it is intended to help the reader's awareness of legal issues and to stimulate further study of the subject as necessary. The law in this area is highly complex and its application to specific situations requires careful consideration. The following notes should not, therefore, be relied upon as a substitute for detailed legal advice. The Bibliography contains references to a number of texts on the subject. The following is based on English Law, that is the laws applying to England and Wales. The law may differ in Scotland, the European Community and other countries throughout the world.

Engineers and the Law

Many engineers working in the manufacturing, process, construction or service industries may well feel remote from the law in their day-to-day work. Any matter involving legislation may be handled by the company's management. Engineers may well ask 'why is there a need for the Code, and how does it apply to me?' From studies of recent accidents and incidents, as well as by making comparisons with other professions (e.g. the medical profession), it is evident that there is a growing likelihood of 'professionals' being made legally accountable for their actions.

Consequently, all engineers need to acquire an understanding of the law and its relevance to risk issues. An outline guide to relevant aspects of the law is illustrated in Figure 3.

Your duty is to know the law as it applies to you. The legal requirements are a minimum standard. Furthermore, although the Civil Law is the judge of some aspects of professional services, there are many instances where the Criminal Law may apply. At the extreme, accidental loss of life could result in the charge of manslaughter. This depends on establishing, in many cases, proof of reckless disregard of accepted practices or of conscious wrong-doing. Less serious criminal offences may involve strict or absolute liability to which there is a defence only in very limited circumstances. Engineers should therefore seek appropriate professional advice at an early stage if they have doubts about the application of the law or regulations in a particular situation.

Example of legislation affecting the work of engineers

One example of the impact of the law affecting the work of engineers is from legislation imposed by government through the agency of the Health and Safety Executive. For instance, *The Health and Safety at Work Act (1974)* and its associated regulations, impose duties on persons who design, manufacture, import or supply articles for use at work to ensure, so far as is reasonably practicable, that they are safe, and to test them, provide proper information, carry out research with a view to the elimination of risks and to carry out other duties. This Act also imposes other duties on employers and persons at work.

An in-depth assessment from first principles and a cost/benefit analysis are not needed for every job. The extent of consideration should match the nature of the hazard and the extent and uncertainty of the risk and the measures necessary to avert it. In many cases it will be sufficient to identify and comply with the appropriate British or International Standard or Code of Practice. However, actions may be challenged by others with hindsight and an engineer may have to establish the facts in the face of a hostile situation. Ultimately, a decision may have to be defended on judgement and so, particularly where decisions or recommendations are finely balanced, the consideration should be documented and, if possible, corroborated. There is no substitute for truly professional practice in this regard.

Latest European Directives and relevant UK Regulations

The directives are part of the European Commission's programme of action on health and safety, which is an essential ingredient in the move towards a single European market. They have been developed under an article *(Article 118A)* specially added to the *Treaty of Rome* for this purpose. Most of the primary duties in the new *Health and Safety at Work Regulations* are already addressed in general terms by existing UK legislation. Guidance on the latest regulations is available from HMSO.

Six areas are covered in the most recent package of UK regulations:

- Management of Health and Safety
- Work Equipment Safety
- Manual Handling of Loads
- Workplace Conditions
- Personal Protective Equipment
- Display Screen Equipment.

Others are already in place or will follow in the future. This is in addition to regulations from *Article 100A Directives*, which relate to manufactured products.

Commentary on Figure 3

Criminal Law

This is the Law of Offences (i.e. crimes) against the State and those under its protection, calling for prosecution usually by officials of the State. It arises from the need to maintain law and order. Criminal Law is actionable officially by the prosecution of offenders. A criminal case is normally brought by the State, or rather by the Crown Prosecution Service as the agents of the State, against an individual. However, with certain crimes, an affected member of the public may commence criminal proceedings.

Different terms are used in Criminal and Civil Law and should not be confused. The accused may be prosecuted under Criminal Law whereas a private individual may be sued under Civil Law. In a criminal case, if the accused person is found to be guilty, he or she may be fined or imprisoned; the successful party in a civil case may be awarded damages or granted an injunction.

Administrative Law

This is law which stems from the need for governments to appoint officials to administer various activities and is concerned with the functioning of official agencies providing various services. Businesses operate within such a framework; they must observe planning regulations and comply with employment legislation. It should be noted,

complete correction to the professional satisfaction of the engineer, to an adjustment to the areas of responsibility between the parties which may result, in extreme cases, in the engineer contracting out of further responsibility or abandoning his or her engagement. In cases where the latter course seems a possibility, the engineer should consult his or her professional organisation and seek its advice as well as the advice of an independent legal adviser in a timely manner. A careful record, with corroboration, is always desirable in such extreme circumstances.

Tort

There are various kinds of civil wrongs, or Torts, which enable a person who has sustained an injury or loss to claim damages. An individual or organisation may face action for a variety of Torts e.g. defamation, negligence, nuisance or trespass.

Whilst an engineer's responsibility in contract can (subject to limits imposed by the general law) be defined and regulated by the parties involved, such is not the case with liabilities in Tort (i.e. a civil wrong), which can involve the community as a whole. As a professional, an engineer may owe a duty of care to anyone who may reasonably be expected to be affected by his or her professional conduct.

The professional codes set down benchmarks for services by engineers. These are self-imposed standards against which, in a particular case, it can be determined whether professional responsibilities have been discharged. To depart substantially from them invites question unless it can be demonstrated that such departure conforms to accepted practice by rational analysis.

Ultimately, the Laws of Negligence (which may vary considerably according to the jurisdiction involved) will influence the standards. It is impossible in this publication to give a resumé of these. They may be imposed in the form of obligations of strict liability to which defences are extremely limited or in more general and voluntary concepts of negligent omissions and commissions. Generally speaking, so far as English Law is concerned, it will be necessary to show that there was some 'proximity' between the damage suffered by the claimant and the engineer's acts or omissions and that it was reasonably foreseeable that the engineer's acts or omissions would cause loss to the claimant.

3. CONDUCT

This section discusses 'Conduct', the third point of the ten point Code. It covers professional Codes of Conduct, responsibility to an employer and the resolution of risk concerns.

Professional Institutions' Codes of Conduct

All major Institutions publish Codes of Conduct for their members, setting out the expected standards of professional conduct. These codes apply to conduct which may involve risk issues as well as other situations, and members may be held to account for behaviour which falls short of the required standard. Engineers should therefore be conversant with any Codes of Conduct and Rules produced by their Institution(s), and act accordingly.

The Engineering Council's Code of Conduct

The Engineering Council similarly has a *Code of Conduct* set out in its Bye-Laws. In effect this is the totality of its *Rules of Conduct* which are issued separately. These regulate the conduct of its registrants.

The *Rules of Conduct* cover the totality of a registrant's conduct, but several are directly applicable to risk issues. These are referred to in *Appendix 1*.

The Council also issues Codes of Practice subordinate to its *Rules of Conduct*. Codes of Practice describe the practice which The Engineering Council recommends should be followed by registrants in particular situations. *The Code of Professional Practice on Engineers and Risk Issues* is one such Code of Practice. However, this document, *Guidelines on Risk Issues,* does not have a formal link with the framework outlined overleaf.

11

FIGURE 5   *The Framework of the Rules of Conduct of The Engineering Council*
            (N.B. Bye-Laws 68 and 69 are reproduced in full in *Appendix 1*.)

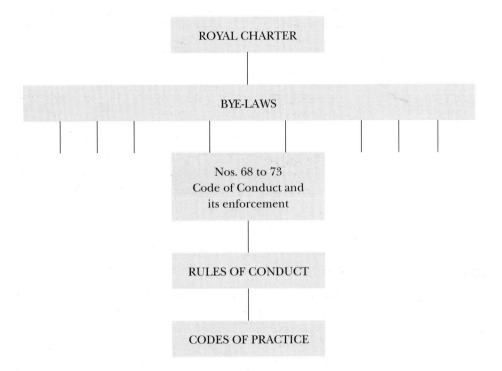

The Code and Rules of Conduct of The Engineering Council and individual Institutions will normally be consistent. The Council's Rules of Conduct and Codes of Practice are intended to embrace all engineering disciplines. However, the professional Institutions may, from time to time, issue rules and codes for their specific disciplines which go further than these general rules.

Resolving a Risk Concern   It is in an organisation's interest to set out a formal procedure for resolving risk concerns. Where a procedure exists, it should be used. In the absence or inadequacy of a procedure, it is recognised that judgement is required. In such situations the following may be helpful:

You, as an engineer, may become aware of a potentially dangerous situation. In the majority of cases, raising the matter informally will result in resolution at local level. Occasionally, however, you might judge that this has not happened and that an unacceptable risk is still being allowed to persist.

A true judgement as to the real level of risk involved is often difficult, as is the subsequent judgement about its acceptability or otherwise. The potential for conflict and the difficulty of making decisions in marginal situations is obvious, especially when the possibility of sanction by your employer, client or Institution is taken into account.

You should therefore have carried out an objective, professional assessment of the level of risk making sure that:

(a) your opinion is truly objective

(b) you understand the wider issues of the organisation's operations

(c) personal motivation is not clouding your judgement

(d) your warning has been properly explained and understood.

Seeking a second opinion is strongly advised to obtain an objective assessment. This should be done in confidence and could be from a colleague, safety representative or informal contact with your Institution or trade union/professional association. (Although if you decide to approach anyone outside your own organisation, you should take great care to preserve confidentiality and, if you are in any doubt as to your duties of confidentiality, you should seek appropriate legal advice.)

If the matter really cannot be resolved at an informal level, then it should be formally communicated in writing to the person in charge of the activity. The formal letter should also be copied to the person with ultimate responsibility for the activity (e.g. Director of Engineering, Director for Safety). There may also be a safety committee set up to consider such matters.

If this does not result in the matter being resolved, then you should re-evaluate it again as above.

Raising the matter outside the organisation is extremely unusual and up to your own conscience. You should recognise that your job may be at risk. Also legal advice should be sought if you have not already done so.

If you decide to go outside the organisation, firstly approach your professional engineering Institution for advice but note the earlier advice on preserving confidentiality. If it is unable to help, where necessary, advice can be sought from The Engineering Council. It should be recognised that the professional Institution and The Engineering Council may offer advice but cannot provide a safeguard. Additionally, you should consider contacting the appropriate regulatory body.

Raising the matter in the public domain is not advocated. Maintain confidentiality at all times and keep to the professional route outlined above.

Guidelines have also been produced by the Royal Academy of Engineering (formerly the Fellowship of Engineering, see *Appendix 4, Bibliography*).

4. APPROACH

Most engineers will have little direct influence over the form of their organisation's risk management programme. An individual's scope for modifying it will inevitably be heavily influenced by site and corporate culture. However, if the culture is not conducive to effective risk management, engineers should not simply accept things as they are, but seek to work actively within the organisation to improve matters.

The following principles expand on this approach:

Work Systematically

A systematic and documented approach will be more cost effective, auditable and more likely to come to the right conclusions. It will also help to prevent communication failures. Individuals may have to defend their decisions in court, and if they cannot demonstrate a systematic approach, they are liable to find this difficult to do. An appropriate level of quality assurance and audit, including proactive* audit of current activities against best practice, is essential for effective risk management. As a minimum, key risk decisions together with the reasoning should be recorded. It should not be an unreasonable burden. If it is unnecessarily bureaucratic the engineer should seek to have the systems modified so that they contribute more cost effectively to improved quality.

Take the Initiative

Engineers should, within the constraints of their work responsibility, seek to identify possible hazards and ways to reduce risk. They should not take the attitude that 'risk management is someone else's business'; rather, they should take the initiative. For example, by trying to make sure that hazardous situations or unsafe practices do not persist. Alternatively, taking the initiative might entail making the manager or employer aware of his or her responsibility. Additionally, engineers should look after their own personal safety, and help others to look after theirs. They should set an example by observing rules and regulations, using protective equipment, etc.

Comply with Regulations

Engineering standards and Codes of Practice can be thought of as the result of generic risk assessments. They are clearly a very cost-effective form of risk assessment; the situation will have been examined at a level of detail and expertise not usually available to individual companies. Compliance can also form a readily understood and testable basis of contractual or regulatory requirements. However, this approach does have

---

* creating or controlling a situation by taking the initiative.

limitations. It is very hard for regulations to cover the interactions of complete systems in complex process plants, for example. It is all too easy to lead to the conclusion that compliance with regulations is all that is required for safety, i.e. compliance ends up taking precedence over the wider considerations of risk management.

The balance of modern thinking in risk assessment and regulation is therefore moving towards a combination of codes and standards with 'goal setting'. This encourages systematic assessment of the whole operation/activity (see References 2 and 4).

Engineers should be aware of the need to balance reliance on codes and standards with project-specific risk assessment. Simply complying with these does not absolve an engineer from his or her broader responsibilities. Loopholes, omissions or ambiguities should not be exploited to gain an advantage incompatible with the effective control of risk.

Ensure Competence

Both from the professional integrity point of view and to avoid legal repercussions, specialist input should be obtained where necessary, even if it has to be 'bought in'. Engineers should not exceed their level of competence where the result might put people at risk, nor ask others to exceed theirs. Similarly, it is important to validate the competence of contractors and sub-contractors.

Recognise Human Factors

Human factors are now known to have an important role in the control of risk. Design using ergonomic principles (see *Appendix 5, Glossary*) involves designing the job, working environment or product to take proper account of human capabilities and fallibilities. It should be recognised that all too often the operational design intent is not followed by those operating or using the design in practice. Engineers should be familiar with these issues and good design practices. Engineers should also have an appreciation of the causes of human errors so that the reasons behind safe operation and design practices can be appreciated (see *Appendix 2*).

FIGURE 6 *Areas Affecting Human Performance*

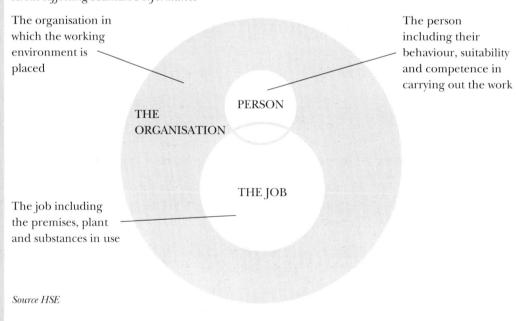

The organisation in which the working environment is placed

The person including their behaviour, suitability and competence in carrying out the work

PERSON

THE ORGANISATION

THE JOB

The job including the premises, plant and substances in use

Source HSE

Human performance is often shown as being influenced by three overlapping areas (Reference 8):

(a) the organisation
(b) the job
(c) personal factors.

The Organisation   The culture of an organisation is often found to be a major influence on risk management issues. *Guideline 7, Management,* discusses this in more detail and sets out examples of good practice.

The Job   Matching the job to the person will ensure that he or she is not overloaded and makes an effective contribution to the enterprise. Physical match includes the design of the whole work place and working environment. Mental match involves the individual's information and decision making requirements, as well as their perception of the tasks. Mis-matches between job requirements and people's capabilities provide potential for human error.

The major considerations in the design of the job include:

(a) identification and analysis of the critical tasks expected of individuals and appraisal of likely errors

(b) evaluation of required operator decision making and the optimum balance between the human and automatic contributions to safety actions

(c) application of ergonomic principles to the design of man-machine interfaces

(d) design and presentation of procedures and operating instructions

(e) organisation and control of the working environment, including the workspace, access for maintenance, lighting, noise and thermal conditions

(f) provision of correct tools, equipment and protective clothing

(g) scheduling of work patterns including shift organisation, control of fatigue and stress and arrangements for emergency operations.

Personal Factors   Every individual is different; individual characteristics influence behaviour in complex and significant ways. Some characteristics such as personality are fixed and largely incapable of modification. Others, such as skills and attitude are able to be modified or enhanced. The key is to match the person to the job and vice versa.

References 9 and 11 provide guidance on good ergonomic design practice. References 7, 8, 10 and 12 provide more information on human factors. Checklists can serve as a useful indicator of the extent to which human factors and ergonomic principles have been taken into account in a particular situation.

Take Care with Computer Software   The benefits of using computers in engineering applications is very substantial indeed in terms of reliability, cost and ease of use. However, if a system is such that an error in the software alone could cause a fault, then care must be taken to ensure that the software is to the standard required by the application.

Quality assurance of software can be achieved by following the principles of ISO 9000, as required by the TickIT scheme. In addition an agreed development process should be used, for instance, as specified in the STARTS Guide.

The use of computers or programmable logic controllers in systems which have a direct impact on safety obviously requires special care. General guidance on this is provided by the Health and Safety Executive.

It has been shown to be virtually impossible to give reliability figures for software when the reliability requirements are less than 1 error in 10^4. This implies that very demanding quality assurance procedures and methods are needed in such circumstances. Some advocate the use of mathematical methods to gain insight into the properties of the software, as specified by the UK Ministry of Defence. Testing is inadequate in almost all cases, since the total number of potential test cases is effectively infinite.

Specific standards for the assessment of software in safety-critical contexts are being developed. For the nuclear industry the standards are agreed and are well advanced in the civil avionics sector and are referenced in the Bibliography. A generic standard is being developed by the International Electrotechnical Commission, but is not yet agreed. It is expected that this standard will form the basis of European certification schemes within the Single Market.

Professional advice on this topic is available from the Institution of Electrical Engineers, and useful background is available from a report undertaken jointly by the Institution of Electrical Engineers and the British Computer Society.

The possibility of malicious damage should be considered, i.e. computer hacking and viruses. Such interference could have widespread implications and plans should be made to mitigate against this possibility.

Appendix 4, Bibliography contains appropriate references.

5. JUDGEMENT

Professional judgement is by far the most important tool in risk management. Judgement is particularly important in the initial assessment of risks and deciding on their tolerability. Formal risk assessment and evaluation methods should be used as aids to judgement, not as substitutes for it. There are many limitations and uncertainties associated with even the most scientific methods. In such situations, it may be prudent to prepare for the worst eventuality by drawing up contingency plans. It should also be recognised that risk data will normally be only one input into business decisions, and many of the other factors will be essentially qualitative. Where the realisation of a hazard could give rise to significant consequences to people and the environment, then specialist advice should be obtained if necessary.

6. COMMUNICATIONS

Many accidents result from communication breakdowns. Frequently someone knows about a hazard, but fails to communicate with those who need to know. All too often, individuals do not recognise or understand their risk management responsibilities. Engineers should take the initiative and look for opportunities to encourage greater awareness of risk issues within their organisation. Where necessary, they should also seek to improve the existing communication systems. Engineers should be aware of the potential for communication breakdowns, especially at internal or external interfaces.

Internal interfaces include those between an engineer and different levels of management, departments or functional groups within the same organisation. An example is the interface between a design engineer and the operators (end users). It is important that the design process does not become divorced from the end users. They should be aware of any risks to which they may be exposed, of any relevant limitations inherent in the design or operating procedures, and of any implications for their conduct.

External interfaces include those with customers (end users), suppliers and contractors. Adequate instructions, manuals and training should be provided for customers. This is very important – otherwise the customer will not know the design intent nor the operational safety limits. Similarly, engineers should seek to ensure that suppliers appreciate the quality and safety requirements of the products/processes which they are supplying. When allocating tasks to contractors, engineers should seek to ensure that their requirements, particularly when safety-related, are communicated to those who will actually carry out the work. Generally, safety and quality requirements should be communicated in writing and it may be appropriate to request a written acknowledgement of receipt.

Engineers should pay particular attention to effective feedback on incidents and 'near misses', so that lessons can be learned. This includes feedback from end users of a product or process. A formal company procedure is recommended which records, analyses and disseminates such information. This is in addition to the legal requirements to report certain accidents (e.g. RIDDOR regulations – see *Appendix 4, Bibliography*).

Those who need to know should be provided with the lessons learned as soon as possible. Others could be informed by the circulation of a regular newsletter. An enlightened company culture which encourages the reporting of incidents and 'near misses' is recommended. A confidential and blame-free system may be appropriate.

7. MANAGEMENT

A major contributory cause of many recent accidents has been shown to be management failure (see *Appendix 3*). Engineers should contribute effectively to risk management within their organisation by doing everything reasonably practicable to ensure that good practice is being followed. This section provides an overview of the various activities that make up a typical risk management programme, and then presents some examples of good practice derived from Engineering Council studies and other sources.

Engineers in managerial positions should therefore recognise that they have enhanced responsibilities in three important respects: the introduction and operation of a proper risk management programme; the effective discharge of their broader duties, so that they do not themselves become a source of risk; and in the making of judgements relating to the tolerability of risk. Consequently, engineers have a primary role in ensuring that the risk management programme itself is managed as effectively as any other business activity.

In most ways, the corporate approach should mirror the individual approach described above, i.e. it should be systematic, planned and integrated with business decision making. The management of change is also an important feature. The development of a corporate culture which deals appropriately with risk is most important. Risk management is made much easier where there is a quality-based culture which emphasises individual responsibility and ownership of problems, and where an atmosphere of 'constructive intolerance' of avoidable risks has been established.

Objectives of Risk Management

Risk management is defined in BS 4778 as 'the process whereby decisions are made to accept a known or assessed risk and/or the implementation of actions to reduce the consequences or probability of occurrence'. The three main activities in a risk management programme are therefore hazard identification, risk assessment and risk control (see Figure 7). These are discussed in turn below, but the objective of risk management should be clarified first: it should contribute to the business objectives and not be allowed to become an end in itself.

Risk management is not simply the reduction of risk, although this is the intended result. A more realistic objective for many organisations would be to strike an appropriate balance at the conceptual stage between the benefits from reduced risk, the expense of that reduction and the gains from the enterprise. An objective judgement can then be made on how to operate in such a way as to optimise the level of risk on a day-to-day basis. However, some risks may simply be unacceptable and therefore not a matter for compromise or optimisation. As with all other aspects of management, risk management is concerned with setting and achieving goals which support overall company or societal goals.

Component Activities

Hazard identification, risk assessment and risk control are discussed below in relation to a generalised project (see Table 1). The needs of different organisations will vary considerably, according to their complexity and the hazards associated with their operations. The basic approach will apply in all cases, but the degree of formality and the extent of risk assessment and control programmes may fall anywhere between everyday professional judgement and a full safety case.

FIGURE 7   *Risk Management Activities*

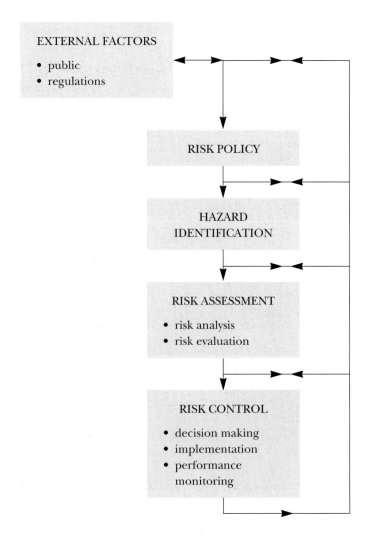

Hazard Identification

It is important to identify hazards systematically. If this is not done then defence against the hazards or management of the risk arising from them can be seriously impaired. There are a number of techniques which ask the necessary 'what if...?' questions systematically. Examples include Hazard and Operability Study (HAZOP), Failure Mode & Effects Analysis (FMEA), and Operational Experience Reviews. These terms are described in the Glossary. References 5 and 6 provide further guidance.

Human error often proves to be a major contributor to overall levels of risk and may deserve specific consideration. Human error identification techniques include task analysis or reference to checklists of potential human errors. If human error is thought to be particularly important then expert advice should be sought.

The potential for common cause and common mode failures should also be considered, e.g. failure of the power supply disables all the safety systems or, as in the case of Chernobyl, they are all overridden.

Risk Assessment   *Risk Analysis*

Having identified the hazards, risk analysis establishes the level of risk in terms of consequences and likelihood. The level of complexity required depends on the type of study. Useful results can often be achieved through simple analysis without resorting to the more sophisticated techniques.

TABLE 1   *The Generalised Project*

PROJECT PHASE	SUB-PHASE	EXAMPLE OF RISK ACTIVITY
PRE-PROJECT	Concept/Feasibility	Policy
		Risk engineering plan
	Statement of Requirements	Basic criteria/goals
		Initial hazard identification
	Technical Specification	and risk assessment
DESIGN AND CONSTRUCTION	Front end design	Hazard identification
	Detailed design	Specific risk assessments
	Procurement	
	Construction	Inspection
		Monitoring
	Pre-commissioning	Follow-up review
OPERATION	Commissioning	Performance monitoring, Audit
	Operation & maintenance	Loss and near-miss reporting
		Follow-up reviews
	Decommissioning and abandonment	

Note that the above processes are iterative

The consequences of a hazard can be expressed either

(a) quantitatively (e.g. injuries, equipment damage) or
(b) qualitatively (e.g. negligible, minor, serious).

See also *Section II, Perception of Risk (page 4)*, which discusses the range of possible consequences.

Similarly, the likelihood or frequency of a hazard can be expressed either

(a) quantitatively (e.g. per year, per operation, per journey) or
(b) qualitatively (e.g. unlikely, occasional, likely).

Techniques include fault tree analysis and event tree analysis (see *Glossary*).

References to the above techniques are provided in the *Bibliography*.

Risk Evaluation

This is the process of determining the tolerability/acceptability of risk. It is a subject in itself and is discussed in *Guideline 8, Evaluation (page 21)*.

Risk Control Risk control is the process of implementing the outputs of the previous stages in order to achieve the desired level of risk, initially in the decision making phase of a project, and subsequently throughout the rest of the project life cycle. No matter how good the analysis, there will be no effect on risk until the recommendations are implemented. The good practice presented in Table 2 and *Appendix 3* addresses many of the factors important to the control of risk.

TABLE 2 *Profile of Good Management Practice – 'The 4 Cs'*

This table lists examples of management practices which have been found to correlate with effective risk management. See also *Appendix 3*.

	APPROACH
COMMITMENT	Recognition by top management that effective risk management is essential to success • risk management is a key business objective, integral with business management • regular board level review of risk management performance • policy of 'compliance as a minimum requirement', positive interface with regulators • formal staff reporting system • operation of QA programme to all activities
CULTURE	Reinforces commitment to quality and success through organisation • individual responsibilities and performance targets clearly allocated • system for monitoring risk management performance (audit) • employee/trade union involvement • risk reduction in conceptual design • positive employee health programmes • emergency preparedness
COMMUNICATIONS	Strong formal and informal networks throughout the organisation • policy well-communicated and reinforced • confidential blame-free accident reporting • effective interfaces with customers, suppliers and contractors • identification and enforcement of 'critical procedures' • use of multi-disciplinary teams (designers, operators, planners, risk specialists)

CONTINUING PROFESSIONAL DEVELOPMENT (CPD)	Systematic approach to updating by education and training on risk issues
	
	• knowledge of – codes and standards
	             – organisational interfaces
	             – legal and financial matters
	• registration of engineers encouraged
	• feedback system from customers and lessons learnt back to design, procedures and staff education/training

Performance monitoring is particularly important, and indicators need to be established to enable both risk and risk management system performance to be monitored, using both actual records of loss and 'near misses' to build up a true picture. Figure 8 is an example of such a study which recorded and classified accidents over a period of time. Comparisons with targets and assumptions then allow remedial measures to be identified if necessary. Where practical, indicators of the performance of individual risk management systems also need to be established, so that the functionality and cost-effectiveness of the various components can be checked. Finally, beyond a certain degree of complexity, a means for formally auditing the complete risk management process will be required.

FIGURE 8   *Accident Ratio Study (Reference 15)*

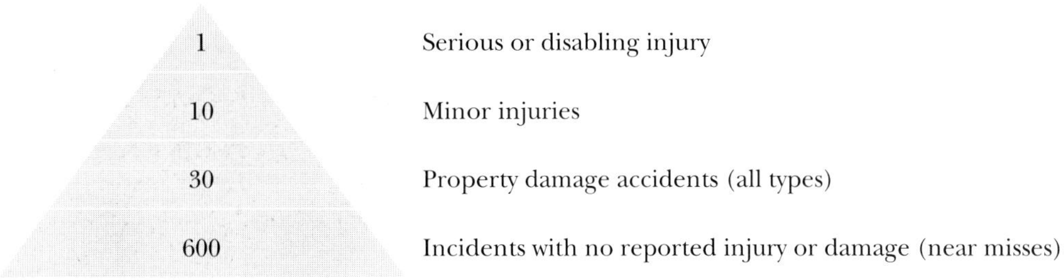

1	Serious or disabling injury
10	Minor injuries
30	Property damage accidents (all types)
600	Incidents with no reported injury or damage (near misses)

Good Practice in Risk Management

The Engineering Council has conducted two studies. The first looked at good practice in risk management through a programme of visits to industrial and commercial organisations (*Appendix 6*), and the second examined the lessons from major accidents. The results of these studies have been combined with those of other work to give a table setting out good practice. Table 2 lists management practices which have been found to correlate with effective risk management. It is not intended to be comprehensive, but should serve to illustrate the approach required.

8. EVALUATION

This process requires judgements to be made based on the output of the risk analysis, i.e. it decides whether or not the level of risk is tolerable. The discussion on the perception of risk in *Section II* illustrates what a difficult area this is. References 1 to 4 provide further guidance. In most cases, the balance is struck on the basis of judgement and experience. All the factors involved are rarely explicit. There are, however, methods for making the basis of decision explicit. These range from qualitative checklists through to multi-attribute analysis (see *Appendix 5, Glossary*), although even the apparently purely qualitative approaches must embody some implicit cost/benefit balance.

ALARP (As Low As Reasonably Practicable)

The ALARP principle is the most commonly used although there are others. It states that risks to individuals and society should be As Low As Reasonably Practicable.

Reference 2 and Figure 9 explain HSE's views of how ALARP fits into an overall approach to risk control. Risks above a certain high level are intolerable and their causes are often prohibited by legislation. At the other end of the scale, there is a very low level of risk which is clearly negligible. Between these two levels, risks are tolerable providing that it can be demonstrated that the cost (in time, trouble and expense) of reducing the risk further would be 'disproportionate' to any improvement achieved.

FIGURE 9   *The ALARP Principle*

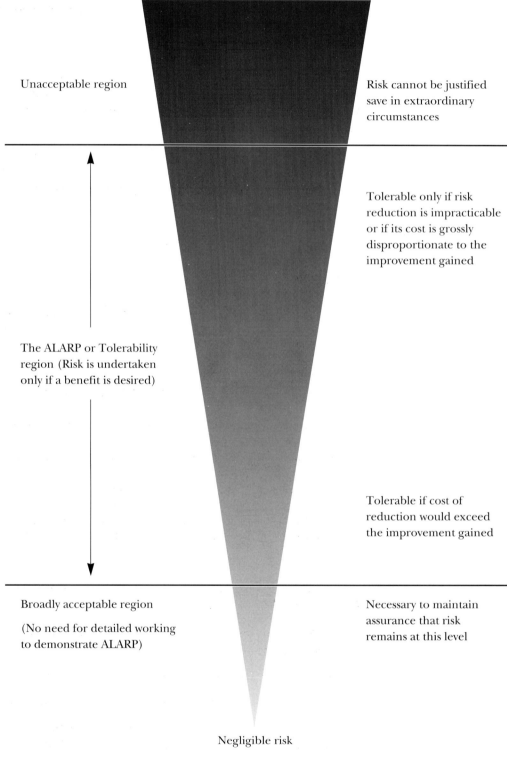

Unacceptable region — Risk cannot be justified save in extraordinary circumstances

The ALARP or Tolerability region (Risk is undertaken only if a benefit is desired) — Tolerable only if risk reduction is impracticable or if its cost is grossly disproportionate to the improvement gained

Tolerable if cost of reduction would exceed the improvement gained

Broadly acceptable region

(No need for detailed working to demonstrate ALARP) — Necessary to maintain assurance that risk remains at this level

Negligible risk

Source HSE

Individual and Societal Risk

Individual risk is defined by The Institution of Chemical Engineers as 'the frequency at which an individual may be expected to sustain a given level of harm from the realisation of specified hazards'. It is usually calculated for the typical average person of the group at risk.

Individual risks vary greatly from job to job and from industry to industry. Table 3 illustrates this.

Societal risk is defined by IChemE as 'the relationship between frequency and the number of people suffering from a specified level of harm in a given population from the realisation of specified hazards'. In other words, it is a measure of the scale and likelihood of a large accident.

Whilst there is broad agreement on individual risk guideline figures it is difficult to do the same for societal risk. Studies in this area to date suggest that there is no readily deducible and uniformly applicable upper level of societal risk. Reference 4 provides further guidance.

TABLE 3 *Levels of Fatal Risk in the UK (average, approximate figures).*

PER ANNUM	
1 in 100	risk of death from five hours of solo rock climbing every weekend[1]
1 in 1000	risk of death in high risk groups within relatively risky industries such as mining[1]
1 in 10,000	general risk of death in a traffic accident[1]
1 in 100,000	risk of death in an accident at work in the very safest parts of industry[1]
1 in 1 million	risk of death in a fire caused by a cooking appliance in the home[2]
1 in 10 million	risk of death by lightning[1]

[1] *The Tolerability of Risk from Nuclear Power Stations.* HMSO 1992.
[2] *Fire Statistics United Kingdom 1988.* Home Office 1990.

Interpreting Risk Assessments

When making risk decisions, particularly based on quantified risk assessments, the following should be recognised:

○ there will be difficulty in obtaining input data and uncertainty in it; consider sensitivity analysis

○ pessimism/conservatism is often used in assessments

○ examine the assumptions, approximations and units used carefully

○ there may be a tendency to concentrate on the numbers; other factors also have an input into the tolerability decision process (see *Section II, Perception of Risk (page 4)*)

○ care should be taken when comparing risk across industries and when comparing risk figures of an existing process against those of a proposed new process.

9. PROFESSIONAL DEVELOPMENT

Training and professional development increase the awareness of risk issues. The overall framework is illustrated below.

FIGURE 10   *The Development of Risk Awareness*

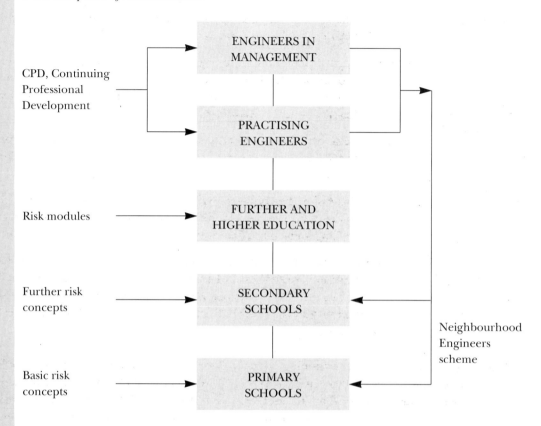

Schools

Children are the public and engineers of the future; risk awareness has many practical benefits for their own safety. The objective should be an introduction to risk issues. All engineers should therefore seek to encourage an appropriate and balanced treatment of risk issues within schools, in their role as professionals, as parents, or as employers. Risk issues should be made as relevant as possible. They could be raised and put into perspective by talking about everyday activities: crossing the road, driving a car, smoking or drinking alcohol.

The Neighbourhood Engineers scheme, organised by The Engineering Council, links registered engineers and technicians with local secondary schools. Working in teams with teachers, Neighbourhood Engineers provide friendly, informal, practical and committed support to schools.

The Engineering Council is currently preparing resource packs to be used by teachers. These will provide background information and teaching aids. The Engineering Council also operates the Technology Enhancement Programme which is for 14–19 year olds and aims to increase capability in technology, mathematics and science, developing skills that are matched to the needs of industry. Another organisation offering teaching aids is SATIS, Science and Technology in Society. Their address is given in the Bibliography.

Further and Higher Education

Education and training on risk issues should be an integral part of every engineer's education. The objective is to instil an awareness of risk issues and basic methods of risk management. The problems of over-crowded teaching programmes and the difficulties this brings for students and staff are recognised. Nevertheless, it is believed that space must be made for the subject to be covered. Additionally, the inclusion of a basic awareness of risk issues into other related courses is encouraged.

24

A possible list of topics for inclusion in a suitable course is suggested below. Many variants will be possible and the level of detail will depend on the nature of the courses involved. It is intended that the topics listed will be included in the syllabuses of both degree (or equivalent) and non-degree courses.

- Changing perceptions of risk; human safety; environmental risks; financial risks; balancing risks and benefits.

- Legal aspects and insurance: the role of The Engineering Council and of the professional Institutions; relevant Codes; legal responsibilities of employers and engineers; relevant legislation (e.g. the *Health and Safety at Work Act*, Employers' Liability and *Consumer Protection Acts*).

- Basic principles of risk assessment: handling uncertainty; preparing safety cases; hazard and operability studies (HAZOPs); determining standards; allocating resources to risk assessment; employing consultants.

- Professional responsibility for managing risk; examples where management has been inadequate; the need for an organised approach; responsibilities of safety officers; making and using safety audits and regular reviews; Total Quality Management.

A suggested time allocation within a degree course is 4 one-hour lectures, supported by 2 four-hour case studies, and 1 four-hour exercise (to make a simple HAZOP or FMEA study), a total of 16 hours per student. This teaching should be available to every engineering student, in all disciplines. Preferably it should take place towards the end of their course.

Practising Engineers and Engineers in Management

Effective training is essential to success in almost every area of engineering, and risk management is no exception. The key to quality and efficiency is professionalism, which is a combination of expertise and attitude. Training and experience provide the expertise, whilst company culture and experience shape the attitudes.

Engineers should have regular opportunities for Continuing Professional Development (CPD) on the assessment and management of risk and on changes in the law. This can be fulfilled mainly by attendance at short courses, conferences and lectures. Responsibility for organising these falls to the higher-education sector, to the Engineering Institutions, to industry, and to specialists in the field.

The development of such further educational and training opportunities is encouraged and engineering employers should ensure that their staff have the time to keep up-to-date in this way. Similarly, all engineers should seek to ensure that they receive the education and training they need, and that those working for them are also suitably developed.

10. PUBLIC AWARENESS

Implications of Improved Public Awareness

The public should be protected from unacceptable risks. They and their elected representatives also have, implicitly or explicitly, a major impact on the way companies and individual engineers make decisions on risk issues. Public perception eventually results in regulation, in media treatment, in planning consents, and in government decisions affecting industry. However, public perception of risk is often at odds with the objective measures used by engineers. Thus engineers should learn about how the public perceives risk and makes risk decisions. Conversely, engineers should, where appropriate, inform the public about how the profession perceives risk and makes risk decisions.

Public Perception of the Profession

Public perception of the engineering profession depends on an engineer's motives in safety and environmental issues being understood. An engineer may be seen as a threat to society when designing a plant which generates toxic waste, but to be protecting society if working on a flood prevention scheme. Reality is often more complex.

Engineers who act with professional integrity when deciding on the tolerability of risk, e.g. about the safe handling of dangerous substances, can be acting for society, not against it. Engineers thus need to explain their role to encourage a more positive view of the profession. Care should be taken to avoid misinterpretation and misconception. Professional public relations advice is recommended.

Public Awareness of Risk Issues

It is usually beneficial for organisations whose activities involve some degree of risk to the public to establish two-way communication on the issues. Early consultation and on-going dialogue help organisations to:

• understand local and community concerns

• take action to respond to these concerns.

This benefits all parties.

Open and honest communication and consultation with the public on risk issues builds trust. Increased identification and understanding between an organisation, its workers, neighbours and the public or allowing them to benefit from the activity, increases the understanding and acceptance of risk.

Well planned and practised emergency procedures for major hazards require pre-arrangements with local authorities and emergency services. They should include plans to communicate with the public and media. Such communications should be clear and unambiguous. The main aim of emergency planning is to reduce risk to people, equipment and the environment. However, arrangements should also be planned to control corporate risk. The arrangements should involve and be prepared in consultation with senior management, engineers, public relations professionals and others as appropriate.

LIST OF RELEVANT ENGINEERING COUNCIL BYE-LAWS AND RULES OF CONDUCT

The following is an extract from The Engineering Council Bye-Laws and Rules which are relevant to the enhancement of registrants' risk awareness. The list is comprehensive and correct at the time of publication, but additions and deletions may occur from time to time. Registrants should maintain a current knowledge of the Council's Bye-Laws and Rules.

Bye-Laws Nos 68 & 69
Code of Conduct and its Enforcement

68 *The Council shall provide a Code of Conduct regulating the activities and conduct of individuals on the Register through the promulgation, from time to time, of Rules of Conduct, which shall prescribe standards of conduct with which failure to comply constitutes misconduct for the purposes of the Charter. The Council may also from time to time promulgate Codes of Practice if it is of the opinion that such codes will further the objects of the Council. The Rules of Conduct and Codes of Practice may be amended, varied or rescinded as the Council may think fit and the Council may, in its absolute discretion, waive the provisions of any of the Rules of Conduct or Codes of Practice for a particular purpose or purposes expressed in such waiver and may revoke any waiver.*

The Council may provide for the appointment of an ethics committee to administer, and give guidance on, the application of the Rules of Conduct and Codes of Practice and the provisions of Bye-Laws 26 to 28 (inclusive) shall apply to such committee.

69 *All individuals on the Register shall be required to conform to the Rules of Conduct promulgated by the Council. Failure by an individual on the Register to comply with such rules shall constitute misconduct for the purposes of the Charter rendering such individual liable to disciplinary action pursuant to Bye-Laws 70 to 73 (inclusive).*

The Council may provide that the provisions of any Codes of Practice promulgated by it shall be available to and shall be taken into account by the investigating and disciplinary bodies and, if appropriate, the appeals committee in determining whether or not an individual on the Register has failed to comply with the Rules of Conduct or is otherwise liable to disciplinary action pursuant to the Charter. The Council may further provide that compliance with the provisions of the Codes of Practice by any individual on the Register shall be a defence against any complaint in any proceedings brought against such individual pursuant to Bye-Law 70 provided that the provisions of the Code of Practice are, in the opinion of the Council, relevant to the complaint being investigated and adjudicated upon.

Complete copies of The Engineering Council's Bye-Laws are available on request.

 APPENDIX 1

RULES OF CONDUCT

Section 1:
Rules likely to be of
relevance to all registrants

Rule No 1   General
Rule No 2   Professional Integrity
Rule No 3   Obtaining and Accepting Work
Rule No 4   Confidentiality
Rule No 5   Contracts with Third Parties
Rule No 6   Performance of Work
Rule No 7   Membership of Other Professional Bodies, Trade Unions and Other Organisations
Rule No 8   Technical Development & Training
Rule No 9   Practice Overseas
Rule No 10 Discipline
Rule No 11 Responsibility for Acts and Omissions of Others
Rule No 12 Engineering Titles and Descriptions

Section 2:
Rules likely to be of
relevance to registrants
in private practice

Rule No 13 Obtaining Instructions from a Client
Rule No 14 Inducements for the Introduction of Clients
Rule No 15 Publicity & Advertising
Rule No 16 Site Boards
Rule No 17 Fees and Assignments
Rule No 18 Conflict of Interest
Rule No 19 Clients' Monies
Rule No 20 Composition of Practices
Rule No 21 Practice Names & Collective Use of Titles and Descriptions
Rule No 22 Managerial Responsibility

Section 3:
Supplementary

Rule No 23 Waivers
Rule No 24 Restrictive Trade Practices Act 1976

Copies of the above are available on request from The Engineering Council.

SOME CAUSES OF HUMAN ERRORS

This appendix is a list of some causes of human errors. It is not a complete list. It should be noted that the list relates mainly to operator/worker errors as opposed to management/organisational errors. The intention is to give an appreciation of causes of human errors so that the reasons behind safe operation and design practices can be appreciated.

Inadequate information

People do not make errors merely because they are careless or inattentive. Often they have understandable (albeit incorrect) reasons for acting in the way they did. One common reason is ignorance of the processes in which they are involved and of the potential consequences of their actions.

Poor communications

Lack of understanding often arises through failure to communicate accurately and fully describe the state of the process. This is particularly liable to occur on shift handovers.

Inadequate design

Designers of plant, processes or systems of work must always take into account human fallibility and never presume that those who operate or maintain plant or systems have a full and continuous appreciation of essential features. Indeed failure to consider such matters is itself an aspect of human error.

Where it cannot be entirely eliminated, human error must be made evident or difficult. Compliance with safety precautions must be made easy. Adequate information as to hazards must be provided. Systems should 'fail safe', i.e. refuse to work in unsafe modes of operation.

Lapses of attention

The individual's intentions and objectives are correct and the proper course of action is selected but a slip occurs in performing it. This may be due to competing demands for (limited) attention. Paradoxically, the highly-skilled performer, because he or she depends on finely tuned allocation of his or her attention to avoid having to think carefully about every minor detail may be likely to make a slip.

Mistaken actions

Doing the wrong thing under the impression that it is right. For example, the individual knows what needs to be done but chooses an inappropriate method to achieve it.

Mis-perceptions

Mis-perceptions tend to occur when an individual's limited capacity to give attention to competing information under stress produces tunnel vision or when a preconceived diagnosis blocks out sources of inconsistent information.

Mistaken priorities

An organisation's objectives, particularly the relative priorities of different goals, may not be clearly conveyed to or understood by individuals. A crucial area of potential conflict is between safety and other objectives such as output or the saving of cost and time.

Wilfulness

Wilfully disregarding safety rules is rarely a primary cause of incidents. Sometimes, however, there is only a fine line between 'mistaken priorities' and 'wilfulness'. Managers need to be alert to the influences that in combination persuade staff to take (and condone others taking) short cuts through the safety rules and procedures because, mistakenly, the perceived benefits outweigh the risks, and they have perhaps got away with it in the past.

 APPENDIX 3

LESSONS FROM PAST DISASTERS

Much can be learnt from past disasters. As well as identifying the contributory causes of a specific disaster, it is important to look at the positive actions taken afterwards. These positive actions can be thought of as good practice in risk management.

In each case, the examples in this Appendix have been produced with reference to the respective official accident reports from which any quotations have been taken. Inevitably some para-phrasing has taken place; it is not practical to list every contributory cause nor every action taken afterwards. The Bibliography references the official accident reports from which a full account of each accident can be gained.

HILLSBOROUGH FOOTBALL STADIUM DISASTER
15.4.89

Severe overcrowding at a football match.

95 died

Contributory Causes

(a) maximum safe capacities were not laid down
(b) entry into individual pens was not controlled numerically
(c) visual monitoring of crowd density was not effective
(d) the capacity of the turnstiles was exceeded.

Actions taken afterwards

(a) planned replacement of standing by all-seating accommodation
(b) *Home Office Guide to Safety at Sports Grounds (Green Guide) revised*; crowd density reduced; turnstile capacity regulated
(c) specific practical actions taken by clubs, e.g.
    – turnstiles inspected and flow rate measured
    – CCTVs installed etc.
    – stewards aged 18-55
(d) Local Authorities to review safety certificates at least once annually
(e) Football Association/Football League established Advisory Design Council.

Quote

… there is no point in holding inquiries or publishing guidance unless the recommendations are followed diligently.

KEGWORTH M1 AIR DISASTER
8.1.89

Aircraft crash. A problem developed in the no. 1 engine. The operating crew mistakenly shut down the no. 2 engine.

47 died

Contributory causes

(a) the nature of the fault was 'outside their training and experience'
(b) the operating crew 'reacted to the initial problem prematurely and in a way contrary to their training'
(c) there was coincidental positive reinforcement that indicated shutting down the no. 2 engine was the correct course of action.

Actions taken afterwards

(a) examination of the monitoring circuitry for left/right sensing
(b) disseminate information on vibration problems, amend flight manuals
(c) vibration indicators to have an 'attention getting facility', i.e. high alarm
(d) consider inspection procedures which could lead to early detection of damage that could lead to failure of a blade
(e) research the practicality of external closed circuit TV monitoring.

Quote

It is much easier to advocate such a policy (i.e. to avoid making hasty decisions) on the ground than it is to execute it in the air when presented with an unusual emergency.

 APPENDIX 3

CLAPHAM RAIL CRASH	**Three trains collided due to a signalling fault.**
12.12.88	35 died

Contributory Causes
(a) degradation of working practices, quality of supervision, quality of testing, training, allocation of meaningful job descriptions, communication to workforce of standards for testing and installation work, supply of accurate drawings
(b) there was no effective system for weekend working to limit excessive hours, ensure availability of appropriately qualified staff and no overall timetable
(c) the potential for the wiring fault had not been identified (hazard identification)
(d) lessons were not learnt from past incidents.

Actions taken afterwards
(a) introduction of TQM and BS 5750 systems
(b) pay and conditions restructuring to modern salaried approach which included quality achievement payments
(c) training and certification of competence; this includes identifying training needs, distance learning and introduction of licensing to practice and certification schemes for workforce
(d) audit and management surveillance; line management of safety assessed under the International Safety Rating System (ISRS).

Quote *There was a total failure to communicate effectively both up and down the lines of management.*

PIPER ALPHA	**Fire on North Sea oil platform.**
6.7.88	167 died

Contributory causes
(a) breakdown in communications and Permit to Work system at shift changeover
(b) the initial explosion put the main power supplies and the control room out of action
(c) regulations did not require remote but potentially hazardous events to be assessed systematically
(d) the safety policies and procedures were in place; the practice was deficient, e.g. frequency of emergency training.

Actions taken afterwards
(a) regulatory authority transferred from Department of Energy to HSE
(b) requirement within the safety case for the setting of risk reduction goals
(c) safety case to demonstrate that the safety management system is effective, comprehensive, quality assured and auditable
(d) many design requirements, e.g. provision of Emergency Shutdown Valves (ESDVs), Temporary Safe Refuges (TSRs).

Quote *Senior management were too easily satisfied that the Permit to Work system was being operated correctly, relying on the absence of any feedback of problems as indicating that all was well.*

KING'S CROSS UNDERGROUND FIRE
18.11.87

A fire, probably started by a discarded cigarette, rapidly engulfed an escalator on the London underground.

31 died

Contributory Causes

(a) the public continued to smoke despite a ban
(b) maintenance/inspection of the escalators was not performed properly; much of the equipment in the control room was out of order
(c) the member of staff who was first alerted to the fire did not inform his colleagues; Police radios did not work underground
(d) there was no evacuation plan.

Actions taken afterwards

(a) ISRS, International Safety Rating System adopted
(b) formal risk assessment applied to all projects, expenditure and changes in work activities
(c) Safety and Quality Director on Executive Committee
(d) integration of Safety and Quality initiatives into company overall TQM programme
(e) mission statement for customers 'To provide a safe, quick, reliable transportation system of which all can be proud.'

Quote

... lulled into a false sense of security by the fact that no previous escalator fire had caused a death. No one person was charged with the overall responsibility for safety.

HERALD OF FREE ENTERPRISE RO-RO FERRY DISASTER
6.3.87

The ship put to sea with its bow doors open.

188 died

Contributory causes

(a) reporting system to check the doors was not effective
(b) the emergency lighting system failed
(c) 'failure to give clear orders about the duties of officers contributed so greatly to the causes of this disaster.'
(d) 'The voice of the Masters (ship Captains) fell on deaf ears ashore.'

Actions taken afterwards

(a) door open/closed indicator lights fitted on the bridge
(b) emergency lighting system redesigned to operate when immersed and tipped at a severe angle
(c) company standing orders and regulations revised to promote uniformity of practice throughout ships of the fleet
(d) regulations regarding stability calculations reviewed
(e) counting of passengers and crew on board tightened up
(f) research programme to enhance the stability and survivability standards of Ro-Ro passenger ferries.

Quote

It is apparent that the new top management has taken to heart the gravity of this catastrophe and the company has shown a determination to put its house in order.

 APPENDIX 3

CHALLENGER SPACE SHUTTLE DISASTER
28.1.86

Mission 51-L exploded soon after take off.

7 died

Contributory causes

(a) faulty design of a seal unacceptably sensitive to a number of in-service factors.
(b) the sub-contractor's management reversed its position and recommended the launch, contrary to the views of its engineers in order to accommodate a major customer
(c) NASA management structure permitted internal flight safety problems to by-pass key Shuttle managers
(d) the Safety, Reliability and Quality Assurance workforce was reduced partly due to budget and time pressures.

Actions taken afterwards

(a) design re-evaluation included tests over the full range of in-service conditions
(b) formal objective criteria adopted for accepting or rejecting identified risks
(c) Safety, Reliability and Quality Assurance department strengthened and adopted a system for anomaly documentation and resolution which included trend analysis.

Quote

… neither Thiokol nor NASA responded adequately to internal warnings about the faulty seal design.

THE ABBEYSTEAD EXPLOSION
23.5.84

A methane/air explosion occurred at a water pumping station.

16 died

Contributory causes

(a) an unusual design feature allowed methane to accumulate in an enclosed valve house situated underground; a flammable atmosphere had not been envisaged there
(b) a washout valve was not used in accordance with the operating manual provided by the designers
(c) the presence of dissolved methane in water supply systems had not achieved wide circulation amongst civil engineers in the industry.

Actions taken afterwards

(a) design requirements were changed to allow for the safe venting of any methane gas
(b) strict control of the operation of washout valves, e.g. locked closed
(c) the hazard of dissolved methane was widely publicised and incorporated into training courses. HSE published further advice.

Quote

No documentation relating to the changes has been produced, and no guidance on their potential effects appears to have been sought from the designers of the system.

HYATT REGENCY WALKWAYS COLLAPSE KANSAS CITY
17.7.81

Two suspended walkways in a hotel collapsed.

114 died

Contributory causes

(a) the design of the suspension connections did not comply with the relevant Building Code
(b) the decision to change the design was made by telephone, but was not documented.
(c) the structural engineer's design drawings did not clearly assign design responsibility to the steel fabricator
(d) the structural engineer did not review the drawings sent back by the steel fabricator carefully enough.

Actions taken afterwards

(a) responsibilities between project team members regularised
(b) structural engineers reminded that they assume overall responsibility for their designs.

Quote

As indicated by their stamps, these shop drawings were reviewed by the contractor, structural engineer and architect.

FLIXBOROUGH

1.6.74

Vapour cloud explosion at a chemical plant, extensive damage.

28 died

Contributory causes

(a) poor quality control and design of plant modification

(b) due to staff turnover there was no appropriately qualified engineer

(c) there was a large quantity of hot flammable material.

Actions taken afterwards

(a) raised awareness amongst government, industry and the public to the hazards of large chemical plants

(b) policy and assessment branches set up within HSE to co-ordinate and stimulate effort on major hazards

(c) Advisory Committee on Major Hazards (ACMH) set up. This and subsequent work contributed significantly to the current understanding of hazards from chemical plants and lead to special legislation.

Quote

In times of crisis and extreme demand it is easy to overlook the willing horses some of whom may not know their own limitations.

MILFORD HAVEN

BRIDGE COLLAPSE

1970

A box-girder bridge collapsed during erection.

Contributory causes

(a) the design was not strong enough to resist the forces exerted while Span 5-6 was being cantilevered out from Pier 6

(b) the checking procedures were inadequate and failed to reveal the design deficiency.

Actions taken afterwards

(a) similar bridges throughout the country in service, under design and under construction were checked; over 50% required strengthening

(b) the inquiry revealed many failings in all aspects of the design and construction of major steel box-girder bridges, in particular the importance of independent checking and clear allocation of responsibility

(c) a Code of Practice was written

(d) a number of research programmes were instituted and co-ordinated by the Department of the Environment.

Quote

… the excessively mechanical use of Codes of Practice … is unlikely to result in a satisfactory design in the hands of a designer lacking the experience to appreciate and allow for the peculiarities which each individual structure inevitably exhibits.

 APPENDIX 3

RONAN POINT COLLAPSE OF FLATS

16.5.68

A gas leak caused a partial collapse of a block of flats.

4 died

Contributory causes

(a) failure of a substandard brass nut joining a gas cooker to the gas supply resulted in an explosion
(b) the explosion blew out part of a load bearing wall
(c) there was an inherent weakness in the design; the risk of a progressive collapse should have been considered
(d) there was no specific Code of Practice.

Actions taken afterwards

(a) a Code of Practice specific to the type of building was written
(b) Building Regulations dealt with progressive collapse and effect of fire on a building as a whole
(c) Code of Practice on wind loading updated
(d) responsibility allocated to government minister to ensure that Standards and Codes of Practice are kept up to date and new ones issued as necessary.

Quote

They fell victims, along with others, to the belief that if a building complied with the existing building regulations and Codes of Practice it must be deemed to be safe.

THE TITANIC

15.4.12

The 'unsinkable' passenger liner sank on her maiden voyage when she struck an iceberg in the Atlantic.

Over 1500 died

Contributory causes

(a) the usual practice for liners in the vicinity of ice in clear waters was 'to keep course, to maintain the speed and to trust to a sharp look-out to enable them to avoid the danger'
(b) the ship's radio officer was catching up on a backlog of communications; some outgoing messages from passengers took precedence over ice warnings
(c) there were 2,208 people on board with lifeboat accommodation for only 1,178; additionally many lifeboats left partially filled.

Actions taken afterwards

(a) lifeboat or lifeboat and pontoon raft provided for every single person
(b) new rules for watertight bulkheads
(c) all vessels with over 50 persons equipped with a wireless and emergency source of power
(d) rockets to be used only as distress signals
(e) international conference instituted, (SOLAS, Safety of Life at Sea, still in existence today).

Quote

It is hoped that the last has been heard of the practice (see contributory cause (a)) and that for the future it will be abandoned for what we now know to be more prudent and wiser measures.

 APPENDIX 4

REFERENCES AND BIBLIOGRAPHY

This appendix assembles texts relevant to the engineer and risk issues, also listed are some journals and organisations which are concerned with risk issues.

References used in the Text

1 Comments received on The tolerability of risk from nuclear power stations
London: HMSO, 1988, ISBN 011885481X

2 HSE The tolerability of risk from nuclear power stations
London: HMSO, 1992, ISBN 0118863681

3 HSE Risk criteria for land-use planning in the vicinity of major industrial hazards
London: HMSO, 1989, ISBN 0118854917

4 HSE Quantified risk assessment: Its input to decision making
London: HMSO, 1989, ISBN 0118854992

5 HSE Specialist Inspector Report (SIR) 29 Major hazard assessment: a survey of current methodology and information sources.

6 KLETZ, T. A.
Hazop and Hazan: notes on the identification and assessment of hazards
3rd edition, ISBN 0852952856
London: Institution of Chemical Engineers 1992

7 KLETZ, T. A.
An Engineer's View of Human Error
The Institution of Chemical Engineers,
Second edition 1991, ISBN 085295 265 1

8 HSE Human factors in industrial safety, HS(G)48
London: HMSO, ISBN 011885486 0

9 ISO 6385 'Ergonomic principles of the design of work systems'

10 JENKINS, A. M., BREARLEY, S. A. & STEPHENS, P.
Management at risk. SRDA-R4
AEA Technology: 1991, ISBN 0853563624

11 PHEASANT, S. T.
'Ergonomics standards and guidelines for designers'
BSI, ISBN 0580153916

12 McCORMICK, E. J. & SANDERS, M. S.
'Human factors in engineering and design'
McGraw Hill, New York

13 HUMPHREYS, P. (Ed.)
'Human Reliability Assessors Guide'
Produced by the Human Factors in Reliability Group,
Published by the SRD Association, SRDA-R7, 1993

14 HSC Study group on human factors,
Second report, 'Human Reliability Assessment – a critical overview', ISBN 0 11 885695 2

15 BIRD, F. E. Jnr & GERMAIN, G. L.
Practical Loss Control Leadership, 1985

General References

ASSOCIATION OF PROJECT MANAGERS
Project Risk Analysis and Management, March 1992

BERNOLD, T. (Ed.)
Industrial risk management: a life cycle engineering approach. Proceedings of an international conference.
Amsterdam: Elsevier, 1990, ISBN 0444880046

CONFEDERATION OF BRITISH INDUSTRY (CBI).
Developing a safety culture; business for safety.
CBI May 1990, ISBN 0852013612

COOPER, D. F. & CHAPMAN, C. B.
Risk analysis for large projects 1987
London: Wiley, 1987, ISBN 0471912476

COVELLO, V. T.
Effective risk communication: the role and responsibility of government and non-government organisations
Plenum Press, 1989, 365 pp, ISBN 0306430754

COX, S. J. & TAIT, N. R.
Reliability, safety and risk management
Oxford: Butterworth/Heinemann 1991
ISBN 0750610735

GENEVA ASSOCIATION
Annual Conference, since 1983, on Management of Risk in Engineering (MORE)

GRIFFITHS, R. F. (Ed.)
Dealing with risk: planning management and acceptability of technological risk
Manchester: Manchester University Press, 1982
ISBN 0719008948

INSTITUTION OF CHEMICAL ENGINEERS
Nomenclature for hazard and risk assessment
Rugby: I.ChemE., Revised 2nd edition, 1992
ISBN 085295297 X

INSTITUTION OF ELECTRICAL ENGINEERS,
Management and Design Division
Management of Risk, Colloquium May 1987
Stevenage: IEE 1987

INSTITUTION OF ENGINEERS, AUSTRALIA
Are you at risk? Managing expectations 1990

INTERNATIONAL SAFETY GROUP ON RISK ANALYSIS
Risk analysis in the process industries:
report (EFCE publication series 45)
London: Institution of Chemical Engineers, 1985
ISBN 0852951833

LEES, F. P.
Loss Prevention in the Process Industries
London: Butterworth & Co., 1980, ISBN 0408106042

ROYAL SOCIETY
Risk: Analysis, Perception and Management.
London: The Royal Society, 1992, ISBN 0854034976.

STONE AND WEBSTER ENGINEERING CORP,
Risk Assessment and Risk Management for the Chemical Process Industry,
Van Nostrand Reinhold, 1991, ISBN 0442234384.

TERRY, G. J.
Engineering system safety
MEP, 1991 154 pp, ISBN 0852987811

WATT COMMITTEE ON ENERGY
Energy and risk: Proceedings of a conference,
London September 1990
London; Watt Committee on Energy 1991

WORLD BANK
Workshop on safety control and risk management
Karlstad, Sweden. November 1989

Computer Software

BRITISH STANDARDS INSTITUTION
Guide to the assessment of reliability of systems
containing software, DD198: 1991

DEFENCE STANDARD 00-56 (Interim)
Hazard Analysis and Safety Classification of the
Computer and Programmable Electronic System
Elements of Defence Equipment. Issue 1, 1991.

DEPARTMENT OF TRADE AND INDUSTRY
SafeIT: 1: overall approach: a government
consultation document on the safety of computer-
controlled systems. May 1990
SafeIT: 2: standards framework: a government
consultation document on the safety of computer-
controlled systems. May 1990

DEPARTMENT OF TRADE AND INDUSTRY
Guide to Software Quality Management System
Construction and Certification using EN 29001
ISBN 0-9519309-0-7. Feb 1992

see also:
1. Requirements and Technical Concepts for
    Aviation. RTCA SC167/DO-178B. USA
2. European Organisation for Civil Aviation
    Electronics. EUROCAE document ED-12B

DEPARTMENT OF TRADE AND INDUSTRY
STARTS (Software Tools for Application to large
Real-Time Systems) Purchasers handbook, second
edition, DTI, May 1989

HEALTH AND SAFETY EXECUTIVE
Programmable Electronic Systems in Safety-Related
Applications.
1. An introductory guide. ISBN 0118839136
2. General technical guidelines. ISBN 0118839063
London HMSO.

INTERIM DEFENCE STANDARD 00-55
The Procurement of Safety Critical Software in
Defence Equipment, Ministry of Defence (Part 1:
Requirements; Part 2: Guidance). April 1991

INTERNATIONAL ELECTROCHEMICAL
COMMISSION
Software for computers in the application of
industrially related systems.
Geneva: IEC

INTERNATIONAL ELECTROCHEMICAL
COMMISSION. 880:86
Software for computers in the safety systems of
nuclear power stations. 1986

INSTITUTION OF ELECTRICAL ENGINEERS
Safety-related systems: a professional brief for the
engineer. London: IEE

WICHMANN, B. A. (Ed.)
Software in Safety-related System. ISBN 0471 93474 7
Wiley. 1992

Contracts

Many of the Engineering Institutions publish model forms of contract. Some of those of
the Civils, Chemicals, Mechanicals and Electronics and Electricals are listed:

I.CIVIL.E
Conditions of contract and forms of tender,
agreement and bond for use in connection with works
of civil engineering construction, 6th edition, 1999
Conditions of contract for design and construction,
1992
Conditions of contract for ground investigation, 1983
Conditions of contract for minor work (<£100,000),
1988

I.CHEM.E
Purple Book, A guide to the I.Chem.E's model forms
of conditions of contract, 1993, ISBN 0852953127
Yellow Book, Sub-contract, 1992, ISBN 085295302X
Green Book, Reimbursable, 1992, ISBN 0852952910
Red Book, Lump-Sum, 1981, ISBN 0852951329

I.MECH.E/I.EEE
MF/1, 1988 reprinted 1989, Home or overseas
contracts with erection including forms of tender,
agreement, sub-contract and performance bond.
MF/2, 1991, Home or overseas contracts for the
supply of electrical or mechanical plant including
forms of tender, agreement, supervision contract,
sub-contract and performance bond.
MF/C, 1978, Home contracts without erection for
electrical and mechanical goods other than
electrical cables.
Commentary on MF/1
Commentary on MF/2

Emergency Planning

GOW, H. B. F. & KAY, R. W.
Emergency planning for industrial hazards.
Barking: Elsevier, 1988 EUR 11591 EN
ISBN 185166260X

KELLER, A. Z. and WILSON, H. C. (Eds)
Disaster prevention, planning and limitation:
proceedings of the first conference,
University of Bradford, September 1989
Published 1990, ISBN 0946655359

KELLER, A. Z. & WILSON, H. C. (Eds)
Emergency planning in the 1990s:
proceedings of the second conference,
University of Bradford, September 1990
Published 1991, ISBN 0946655383

BRITISH SAFETY COUNCIL
Emergency planning and disaster control –
management self-audit

Good Design Practice

BS 4778: 1991 In two parts: Quality vocabulary

BS 7850: 1992 In two parts: Total quality management

BS 5750: In six parts: Quality Systems
London: British Standards Institution

KLETZ, T.
Plant design for safety – a user friendly approach
Hemisphers Publishing, 1991, ISBN 1560320680

PETROSKI, H.
To engineer is human: the role of failure in successful design
London: Macmillan, 1985, ISBN 0333406737

Hazard Analysis

DOW
Dow's fire and explosion index: hazard classification guide.
Fifth edition. American Institute of Chemical Engineers 1981

ICI
The Mond fire, explosion and toxicity index: a development of the Dow index

(FMEA) BS 5760: 1982, Reliability of systems, equipments and components.

See also references 5 and 6.

Human Factors/ Ergonomics

See references 7, 8, 9, 10, 11, 12, 13 and 14

Professional Responsibility

ASSOCIATION OF PROFESSIONAL ENGINEERS OF ONTARIO
Guidelines for a professional engineer's duty to report.
APEO, 1990

FELLOWSHIP OF ENGINEERING
Guidelines on warnings of preventable disasters, 1991

FLORES, A.
Ethics and risk management in engineering
University Press of America, 1990, ISBN 0819175641

Public/Press Relations

EMERGENCY PLANNING COLLEGE
Seminar report on crisis and the media
Easingwold Press No. 2
Home Office, 1991, ISBN 1874321019

REGESTER, M.
Crisis management: what to do when the unthinkable happens
London: Business Books Ltd, 1989, ISBN 009173954 3

Tolerability/ Acceptability

See references 1, 2, 3, 4

Accident Reports
(in date order)

TAYLOR, Lord
The Hillsborough stadium disaster, 15 April 1989, Final Report
London: HMSO, 1989, Cm 962, ISBN 0101096224

TRIMBLE, E. J.
Report on the accident to Boeing 737-400G-OBME near Kegworth, Leicestershire on 8 January 1989.
Air Accidents Investigations Branch.
London: HMSO, 1990, ISBN 0115509860

HIDDEN, A.
Investigation into the Clapham Junction railway accident
London: HMSO, 1989, Cm 820, ISBN 0101082029

CULLEN, Lord
The public enquiry into the Piper Alpha disaster
London: HMSO, 1990, ISBN 010113102X

FENNELL, D.
Investigation into the King's Cross underground fire
London: HMSO, 1987, ISBN 0101049927

SHEEN, Mr JUSTICE
'M. V. Herald of Free Enterprise'. Report of Court No. 8079. Formal investigation.
London: HMSO 1987, ISBN 0115508287

ROGERS, W. P.
Presidential commission on the space shuttle 'Challenger' incident. US, GPO, 1986

HEALTH AND SAFETY EXECUTIVE
The Abbeystead Explosion, A report of the investigation by the Health and Safety Executive into the explosion on 23 May 1984 at the valve house of the Lune/Wyre Water Transfer Scheme at Abbeystead.
London: HMSO, 1985, ISBN 0118837958

US DEPARTMENT OF COMMERCE, NATIONAL BUREAU OF STANDARDS
Investigation of the Kansas City Hyatt Regency Walkways Collapse.
NBS Building Science Series 143
Library of Congress Catalog Card Number: 81-600538-

DEPARTMENT OF EMPLOYMENT
The Flixborough disaster: Report of the Court of Inquiry. London: HMSO, 1975, ISBN 0113610750

MERRISON, A. W.
Inquiry into the Basis of Design and Method of Erection of Steel-Box Girder Bridges (Milford Haven)
London: HMSO, 1973, ISBN 115502793

GRIFFITHS, H., PUGSLEY, A. Sir, SAUNDERS, O. Sir
Collapse of Flats at Ronan Point, Canning Town.
London: HMSO 1968, ISBN 117501212

Lessons Learnt from Past Accidents

EUROPEAN COMMISSION, Joint Research Centre, Institute for Systems Engineering and Informatics, 1991.
Community Documentation Centre on Industrial Risk. Major Accident Reporting System – Lessons To Be Learned From Accidents Notified, G. Drogaris, EUR 13385, CDCIR Reference No: 658-EAb5-IV.3, CD-NA-13385-EN-C, ISBN 92826 22894

HEALTH AND SAFETY EXECUTIVE
HS(R)23 A guide to the Reporting of Injuries, Diseases and Dangerous Occurrences Regulations 1985 (RIDDOR), ISBN 011883858X

HEALTH AND SAFETY EXECUTIVE
HSE 113(L) Your firm's injury records and how to use them.

KLETZ, T. A.
What went wrong? Case studies of process plant disasters.
1988, ISBN 0872019195

TOFT, B. & REYNOLDS, S. A.
Learning from disasters: a management approach
Butterworth Heinemann 1992 (NYP)

Legal References and Standards

JANNER, G.
Everyday Business Law.
Gower Publishing Group, 1989, ISBN 0704506416

KADAR, A., HOYLE, K. & WHITEHEAD, G.
Business Law Made Simple
London: Heinemann, 1984, ISBN 043498597X

PRITCHARD, J.
The Penguin Guide to the Law, ISBN 0140511466

REDGRAVE, A.
Health and Safety
London: Butterworths, 1990, ISBN 0406146012

REDMOND, P. W. D.
General Principles of English Law.
M + E Handbooks, 1991, ISBN 0712110305

NB. There are a large number of supporting regulations in addition to the ones listed below.

Consumer Protection Act 1987
London: HMSO, ISBN 0105443875

Control of Industrial Major Accident Hazards (CIMAH)
SI 1984: 1902 London: HMSO, ISBN 0110479025

Control of Substances Hazardous to Health Regulations (COSHH) 1988
SI 1988: 1657 London: HMSO, ISBN 0110876571

Electricity at Work Regulations 1989
SI 1989: 635 London: HMSO

Environmental Protection Act 1990
London: HMSO, ISBN 0105443905

European Commission Directive on the major accident hazards of certain industrial activities
82/501/EEC Official Journal (L230) 1982

European Commission Directive on the introduction of measures to encourage improvements in the health and safety of workers at work 89/391/EEC Official Journal (L183/1) 1989

Health and Safety at Work Act 1974
London: HMSO, ISBN 0105437743

Sale of Goods Act 1979
London: HMSO, ISBN 0105454796

Unfair Contract Terms Act 1977
London: HMSO, ISBN 0105450774

OECD Council Act
Decision recommendation concerning provision of information to the public and public participation in decision-making processes related to the prevention of, and response to, accidents involving hazardous substances.

OECD Council Act
Decision on the exchange of information concerning accidents capable of causing trans-frontier damage.

Management of Health and Safety at Work Regulations 1992
SI No. 1992 No. 2051, ISBN 0110250516

Journals

Journals published by the Professional Engineering Institutions

BSI News, British Standards Institution, ISSN 0005-3309

Disasters, UNISAF Publications, ISSN 0953-4962

Disaster Management, Blackwells Publishers, ISSN 0361-3666

Fire Prevention

Health and Safety Monitor

Safety Management, ISSN 0951-2624

The Loss Prevention Bulletin, ISSN 0260-9576

 APPENDIX 4

Organisations

British Safety Council,
70 Chancellors Road, London W6 9RS.
Tel: 081-741 1231, Fax: 081-741 4555

Centre of Advanced Litigation (CoAL),
Nottingham Law School,
The Nottingham Trent University,
Burton Street, Nottingham NG1 4BU.
Tel: 0602 418418, Fax: 0602 486489

Confederation of British Industry,
Centre Point, 103 New Oxford Street,
London WC1A 1DU.
Tel: 071-379 7400, Fax: 071-240 1578

Commission of the European Communities.
DG X1.E.1

Fire Protection Association,
140 Aldersgate Street, London EC1A 4HY.
Tel: 071-606 3757, Fax: 071-600 1487

Hazards Forum,
1 Great George Street, London SW1P 3AA.
Tel: 071-222 7722, Fax: 071-222 7500

Health and Safety Executive,
Baynards House, 1 Chepstow Place, London W2 4TF.
Tel: 071-243 6604
also at
St Hugh's House, Stanley Precinct,
Bootle, Liverpool, Merseyside L20 3QY.
Tel: 051-951 4000, Fax: 051-922 5394

Institute of Risk Management,
140 Aldersgate Street, London EC1A 4HY.
Tel: 071-796 2119, Fax: 071-796 2120

Loss Prevention Council,
140 Aldersgate Street, London EC1A 4HY.
Tel: 071-606 1050, Fax: 071-600 1487

Royal Academy of Engineering, (formerly The
Fellowship of Engineering),
2 Little Smith Street, London SW1P 3DL.
Tel: 071-222 2688, Fax: 071-233 0054.

Royal Society for the Prevention of Accidents,
Cannon House, The Priory,
Queensway, Birmingham B4 6BS
Tel: 021-200 2461, Fax: 021-706 8121

Safety and Reliability Society,
Clayton House, 59 Piccadilly, Manchester M1 2AQ.
Tel: 061-228 7824, Fax: 061-236 6977

SATIS (Education in schools), Science and
Technology in Society
The Association for Science Education,
University of Hertfordshire,
College Lane, Hatfield, Hertfordshire AL10 9AA.
Tel: 0707 267411, Fax: 0707 266532

SRD Association, (address from June 1993)
AEA Technology, Thompson House,
Risley, Warrington, Cheshire.
Tel: 0925 254249, Fax: 0925 254569

Trades Union Congress,
Congress House, Great Russell Street,
London WC1B 3LS.
Tel: 071-636 4030, Fax: 071-636 0632

 APPENDIX 5

GLOSSARY

Ergonomics The application of scientific information concerning human beings to the problems of design (Reference 11).

Event Tree Analysis A method for illustrating the intermediate and final outcomes which may arise after the occurrence of a selected initial event (Reference 5).

Fault Tree Analysis A method for representing the logical combinations of various states which lead to a particular outcome (top event) (Reference 5).

FMEA Failure Mode and Effects Analysis
A process for hazard identification where all known failure modes of components or features of a system are considered in turn and undesired outcomes are noted. See BS 5760.

Hazard A situation that could occur during the lifetime of a product, system or plant that has the potential for human injury, damage to property, damage to the environment or economic loss.[1]

HAZOP Hazard and Operability Study
A study carried out by application of guide words to identify all deviations from the design intent with undesired effects for safety or operability, (Reference 6).

Multi-Attribute Analysis A technique designed to encompass factors, such as aversion to low probability accidents and socio-political aspects, which are difficult to quantify in monetary terms. A scoring system for the relevant factors is used based on the judgement of a group of informed people.[3]

Risk A combination of the probability, or frequency, of occurrence of a defined hazard and the magnitude of the consequences of the occurrence.[1]

Risk Analysis Risk analysis is a structured process which identifies both the likelihood and extent of adverse consequences arising from a given activity or facility.

Risk Assessment The integrated analysis of risks inherent to a product, system or plant and their significance in an appropriate context.[1]

Risk Evaluation The appraisal of the significance of a given quantitative (or, when acceptable, qualitative) measure of risk.[1]

Risk Management The process whereby decisions are made to accept a known or assessed risk and/or the implementation of actions to reduce the consequences or probability of occurrence.[1]

Task Analysis A method for identifying and assessing the tasks which humans perform when they interact with a system. It defines the physical actions and thought processes which must be undertaken to perform a task.

Tolerability of Risk A band between the point of maximum tolerability (above which a project must be abandoned altogether) and the point of minimum tolerability (below which a risk is so small that the project can proceed without formal assessment).[3] A 'tolerable risk' is one that society is prepared to live with in order to have certain benefits and in the confidence that the risk is being properly controlled. An 'acceptable risk', which implies that the risk, although present, is generally regarded by those exposed to it as not worth worrying about.

[1] BS 4778: Section 3.1: 1991 Quality Vocabulary
[2] BS Draft 91/89802 Requirements and guidelines for analysis of technological risks
[3] HSE The tolerability of risk from nuclear power stations

ACRONYMS USED IN THE TEXT

ALARP	As Low As is Reasonably Practicable		HSE	Health and Safety Executive
BSI	British Standards Institution		HSWA	Health and Safety at Work Act
CAA	Civil Aviation Authority		QA	Quality Assurance
CPD	Continuing Professional Development		PR	Public Relations
ECRO	Engineering Council Regional Office		TQM	Total Quality Management
HSC	Health and Safety Commission			

 APPENDIX 6

ORGANISATIONS VISITED

Members of the Working Party have taken part in visits to organisations throughout the United Kingdom in order to study examples of good practice. Reports on these visits have been made and from these a number of lessons have been identified which firms that are using risk management systems are likely to find of interest. This information is also of interest to all engineers to help them encourage good practice approaches to the identification and assessment of risk issues.

In publishing this information we wish to acknowledge the help given by the following organisations which were included in the visit programme:

15 March 1991	Lloyds of London
30 April 1991	John Brown plc
30 April 1991	British Nuclear Fuels, BNF plc
22 May 1991	Tarmac Construction
6 June 1991	Comelin UK Ltd
10 September 1991	Information Processing Limited, IPL
9 December 1991	Babcock
23 January 1992	GKN
28 January 1992	Simon Access plc
30 January 1992	Royal Navy Air Station
4 March 1992	Association of Consulting Engineers, ACE
13 April 1992	ICI
23 April 1992	BP Engineering
28 May 1992	Ove Arup and Partners
14 July 1992	Rendel, Palmer and Tritton

MEMBERS OF
WORKING PARTY ON
ENGINEERS AND
RISK ISSUES

Sir William Francis CBE, DSc, LLD, FEng, FICE (Chairman of Working Party)
Chairman, Black Country Development Corporation

Eur. Ing A. C. Barrell BSc, FEng, FIChemE
Chief Executive, Offshore Safety Division, Health and Safety Executive

Dr. R. S. Benson CEng, FIChemE, FIEE
Chief Engineer, International Engineering Technology, ICI Engineering

Mr K. W. Burrage CEng, FIEE, FIRSE, FCIT
Director Engineering Standards, British Railways Board

Mr G. D. Collier BSc
Health & Safety Strategy Branch, Nuclear Electric plc
(also seconded to The Engineering Council for a period)

Group Captain M. Garrigan CEng, FIMechE, RAF (Rtd)
Assistant Director (Technical), Society of British Aerospace Companies

Mr P. Godfrey BSc, CEng, ACGI, MICE, FInst Pet
Director, Sir William Halcrow and Partners Ltd

Mr R. W. Gronbech BSc, CEng, FIMechE
Associate Director, Davy McKee (Sheffield) Ltd

Miss J. C. Hanratty LL B, LL M Hons
Head of BP Insurance, The British Petroleum Co plc

Mr J. L. Hill MA, CEng, MIMechE
Chief Executive, The Loss Prevention Council

Prof. D. E. Newland FEng, FIMechE, FIEE
Department of Engineering, University of Cambridge

Dr. R. P. Pape BSc, FSaRS
Head of Safety Analysis Unit, Offshore Safety Division, HSE

Mr J. T. Stansfeld BSc, CEng, MIMechE
Manager, Safety Technology Department, Lloyd's Register

Dr. A. D. Stephens CEng, FIMechE, MInstMC
Chief Executive, Advanced Robotics Research Limited

Mr I. A. Watson BSc, CEng, MIEE, FSaRS
Consultant formerly with Safety & Reliability Directorate

CO-OPTED MEMBERS
OF TASK GROUPS

Group Captain M. Gilding CEng, MIEE, RAF
Ministry of Defence

Mr J. Reid M Ed, FCII
Senior Lecturer, Glasgow Polytechnic

Mr J. H. Rumley
Engineering Consultant

THE ENGINEERING
COUNCIL STAFF

Mr R. F. Eade BSc, CEng, FIEE, CIMgt
Director, Industry and Regions

Mr S. Morgan BSc, CEng, FIMarE
Senior Executive, Industry

Mr B. Dawkins BSc, CEng, FIEE, FIMechE, MIPM, MIBM
Consultant, Matters of National Importance

Mr E. Coulter MCIM, MIPR
Marketing, Communications and Public Affairs Consultant

Mr K. C. Small MEng, MSaRS
Seconded from Safety Technology Department, Lloyd's Register

Mrs M. Hyde ALA, MII of S
Information Research Consultant

INTRODUCTION

This Code, issued under the provisions of The Engineering Council's Royal Charter, is for the benefit of 290,000 registered engineers and technicians from 44 engineering institutions and aims to encourage greater awareness, understanding and effective management of risk issues. As the code is an umbrella document, the engineering institutions may have additional requirements to suit their particular disciplines. The Code should also help registrants have better regard to public health and safety by taking a lead in the development and introduction of competitive designs, processes and systems that minimise risk.

10 POINT CODE OF PROFESSIONAL PRACTICE ON RISK ISSUES

1.	PROFESSIONAL RESPONSIBILITY	Exercise reasonable professional skill and care
2.	LAW	Know about and comply with the law
3.	CONDUCT	Act in accordance with the codes of conduct
4.	APPROACH	Take a systematic approach to risk issues
5.	JUDGEMENT	Use professional judgement and experience
6.	COMMUNICATION	Communicate within your organisation
7.	MANAGEMENT	Contribute effectively to corporate risk management
8.	EVALUATION	Assess the risk implications of alternatives
9.	PROFESSIONAL DEVELOPMENT	Keep up to date by seeking education and training
10.	PUBLIC AWARENESS	Encourage public understanding of risk issues

ENGINEERS AND RISK ISSUES

Code of Professional Practice

THE ENGINEERING COUNCIL

HSE
Health & Safety Executive

EXPLANATORY NOTES

These explanatory notes amplify the implications of the 10 point Code for individual registered engineers and technicians when dealing with risk issues.

1. PROFESSIONAL RESPONSIBILITY

Exercise reasonable professional skill and care

You have a responsibility to exercise reasonable professional skill and care in the performance of your work.

You have a particular responsibility when forming a judgement about the tolerability of risk.

2. THE LAW

Know about and comply with the law

Keep yourself up to date with the substance and intent of the legal and regulatory framework that applies to your work.

Act at all times in a manner that gives full effect to your obligations under the law and the regulatory framework.

Seek professional advice at an early stage if you have any doubts about the appropriate application of the law or regulations.

3. CONDUCT

Act in accordance with the codes of conduct

Familiarise yourself with The Engineering Council's Code of Conduct, authorised under its Bye-Laws and with any relevant codes provided by your own Institution or professional association.

Act at all times in accordance with the requirements of the appropriate codes of conduct, and recognise that your broader responsibility to society may have to prevail over your personal interests.

Respect your duty of confidentiality to your employer or client, and follow the appropriate procedures within your organisation for raising concerns about potential hazards or risk.

4. APPROACH

Take a systematic approach to risk issues

Risk management should be an integral part of all aspects of engineering activity. It should be conducted systematically and be auditable.

Look for potential hazards, failures and risks associated with your field of work or work-place, and seek to ensure that they are appropriately addressed.

Balance reliance on codes of practice with project-specific risk assessment; be open-minded and do not hide behind regulations.

Do not exceed your level of competence on risk issues or ask others to do so; seek expert assistance where necessary.

5. JUDGEMENT

Use professional judgement and experience

Judgement is required to match the approach to the nature of the hazard and the level of risk. This might vary from a simple assessment to a formal safety case.

Uncertainty is a feature of many aspects of risk management. Be aware of this, and use risk assessment methods as an aid to judgement, not as a substitute for it.

6. COMMUNICATION

Communicate within your organisation

Communicate effectively with colleagues, both up and down the chain of responsibility, to help ensure that risk management activities are sufficiently comprehensive and understood.

Endeavour to raise awareness of potential hazards and risk issues among your colleagues.

Seek to ensure that all those involved with a project are aware of any risks to which they may be exposed, of any relevant limitations inherent in the design or operating procedures, and of any implications for their conduct.

Discuss the reasons for incidents and near misses with your colleagues, so that the lessons can be learned.

7. MANAGEMENT

Contribute effectively to corporate risk management

Help to promote a culture within your organisation which strives for continuous improvement, securing involvement and participation in risk management at all levels.

Give due attention to risk analysis, evaluation, decision making, implementation and monitoring during all phases of an engineering project to ensure effective management of risk.

Seek to ensure that management systems do not allow risk issues to be ignored, subverted or delegated to levels which have no control.

Consider the cost implications of all aspects of risk management.

PEOPLE AND ORGANISATIONS INTERESTED IN THE CODE

Engineers

Employers

Managers

Trade Unions

Government

Professional Institutions

Higher Educational Institutions

Schools

General Public

CODE OF PROFESSIONAL PRACTICE

The Engineering Council
10 Maltravers Street,
London WC2R 3ER

Tel: 071-240 7891
Fax: 071-240 7517

October 1992

The Engineering Council expects registrants to adhere to good engineering practice wherever and whenever possible and considers that this Code of Professional Practice will assist registrants in achieving this standard.

Registrants should be aware that non-compliance with the provisions of this Code may be relevant when considering professional disciplinary matters although adherence to the Code will be regarded as demonstrating good practice which could constitute the best protection against such action. While a failure to adhere to the provisions of this Code by an individual registrant may not necessarily amount to negligence or a breach of an implied contractual term by that registrant, such a failure may evidence an infringement of the Council's Rules of Conduct which could lead to disciplinary proceedings.

This code will come into effect on 1st March 1993.

The provisions of this Code are not intended to form part of any contract entered into between registrants and third parties unless expressly incorporated into such contract and should not be regarded as creating a collateral contract between registrants and third parties.

© The Engineering Council 1992

Printed in the UK by LR Printing Services Limited
295m 10/92.1

---

8. EVALUATION

Assess the risk implications of alternatives

Always consider the possibility of reducing or avoiding a source of risk completely.

The tolerability of risk will vary with context, and the basis for establishing it needs to be understood.

In determining the tolerability or otherwise of a given risk, promote effective consultation with those who may be exposed, where this is practical.

Some risks are any circumstances, while others are so low that they can be tolerated without further justification; between these extremes, assessment is needed.

Some risks are so great that they cannot be tolerated under any circumstances, while others are so low that they can be tolerated without further justification; between these extremes, assessment is needed.

9. PROFESSIONAL DEVELOPMENT

Keep up to date by seeking education and training

Risk issues and approaches to risk management should be integrated into every engineer's initial education and training.

As part of your continuing professional development, seek education and training in risk management techniques.

Increase your awareness of the range of potential hazards and learn from past events.

10. PUBLIC AWARENESS

Encourage public understanding of risk issues

Contribute to the education of the public where you have the opportunity, so that they can be aware of and form an objective and informed view on major risk issues.

Seek to encourage a positive public perception of the engineer's role in the management of risk.

Contribute to improved communication on risk issues between your organisation and the community.

 INDEX